D0524672

TEXAS ALPHABET

TEXAS ALPHABET

Written and Illustrated by JAMES RICE

PELICAN PUBLISHING COMPANY
Gretna 1992

First printing: April 1988
Second printing: November 1989
Third printing: September 1992

Library of Congress Cataloging-in-Publication Data

Rice, James, 1934-
 Texas alphabet/by James Rice.
  p. cm.
 Summary: Introduces words and names, from A to Z,
significant to Texas history, beginning with Austin and
concluding with Lorenzo De Zavala.
 ISBN: 0-88289-692-X
 1. Texas—History—Juvenile literature. 2. English
language—Alphabet—Juvenile literature. [1. Texas—
History. 2. Alphabet.]
I. Title.
F386.3.R53 1988
976.4—dc19
[E]
                                                      87-31159
                                                         CIP
                                                          AC

Printed in Hong Kong

Published by Pelican Publishing Company, Inc.
1101 Monroe Street, Gretna, Louisiana 70053

A is for Austin. Moses Austin started to move American colonists to Texas. His son Stephen continued the work after Moses died.

Texas Jack sez it's a shame poor old Steve froze to death in an unheated East Texas shack before he could finish.

**A** is for Alamo, where brave men fought and died, buying time for Sam Houston to gather the forces to win Texas's independence.

Texas Jack sez he never seen so many Mexicans in all his life.

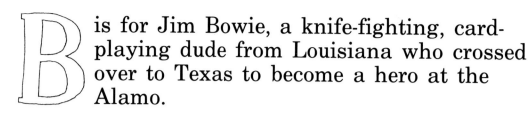

B is for Jim Bowie, a knife-fighting, card-playing dude from Louisiana who crossed over to Texas to become a hero at the Alamo.

Texas Jack sez that nobody told Jim to cut the cards—when he cut 'em, he cut 'em.

is for Sam Bass, a real hard case who took what he wanted with a gun until he got cornered near Round Rock.

C is for Comanche, the best light cavalry in history, and probably the fiercest, if you go by what the old settlers said.

Texas Jack sez he'll stay out of their way anytime.

C is for Davy Crockett, who got tired of the Tennessee hills and came down to Texas to join the scrap at the Alamo.

Texas Jack sez some people just don't know when to leave well enough alone.

is for Ponce de Leon, an early Spanish explorer who was largely responsible for Spain's decision to establish missions and military posts in Texas.

Texas Jack sez the Spaniards' influence can still be seen in Texas today.

E is for empresario, what the Mexicans called those first Texas colonists.

Texas Jack sez it took awhile to talk people into coming to Texas but once they started they couldn't be stopped.

F is for farmer, what most of the colonists called themselves.

G is for Goliad, where 330 Texas prisoners were executed by the Mexicans. But it backfired: the Mexicans' acts at the Alamo and Goliad only hardened the Texans' resolve and galvanized them into action. "Remember the Alamo" and "Remember Goliad" became rallying cries.

Texas Jack sez Goliad didn't work out too good for either side. Texans would forevermore think twice about surrendering after that.

 **H** is for Sam Houston, who finally routed Santa Anna's troops at San Jacinto.

Texas Jack sez old Sam was in everything from soldiering to politics in them days.

I is for *Invincible*, the ship that whisked Santa Anna back to Vera Cruz, Mexico after San Jacinto.

Texas Jack sez he bet old Santa Anna came to wish he'd never left home in the first place.

J is for jackrabbit, who really isn't a rabbit but a hare. He's just about everywhere people aren't in Texas.

Texas Jack sez that, rabbit or hare, he's one of the most underrated critters around.

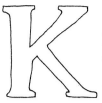**K** is for King Ranch in south Texas, where the famous Santa Gertrudis cattle were developed.

Texas Jack sez they look more like elephants than cattle.

L is for lobo, a Texas wolf howling lonesome on the mesa.

Texas Jack sez they could purely run a cold chill up a body's spine.

M is for mesa, a flat-topped mountain pushing up in the middle of the prairie.

Texas Jack sez it's a good place to climb up and get a view of the lay of the land.

is for nester, who dug his house out of the side of a hill and wrested a living from the ground.

Texas Jack sez them old nesters usually put more into shelter for their animals than for themselves.

O is for oil that keeps wheels turning and fires burning all over the country.

P is for peddler, who brought gossip and merchandise out where there were no stores.

Texas Jack sez some of them peddlers could pert nere sell spurs to sheepherders and tophats to cowboys.

Q is for Quivera, Coronado's fabled city of gold.

Texas Jack sez Coronado only found an old, windblown Indian shanty in the Panhandle instead of treasure. An Indian guide lost his head for his deception.

R is for rodeo, where cowboys go to show off how good they are at their jobs.

Texas Jack sez it's more like to show how crazy they are, ridin' that wild, outlaw stock.

S is for San Jacinto, where the tide of war suddenly changed in favor of the Texans.

Texas Jack sez Sam Houston ended Santa Anna's siesta for good that day.

T is for Texas, another word for biggest and best.

U is for United States, where Texas finally wound up after being under five other flags.

Texas Jack sez it sure made an unbeatable combination when they put the two together, and it kind of makes his chest swell with pride to be a part of it.

is for varmint, any one of a number of small, pesky wild critters.

   Texas Jack sez to leave him out, he ain't no varmint.

is for wind that blows forevermore across
the Texas Panhandle, icy cold in the winter
and hot and dry in the summer.

**X** is for XIT, the biggest spread in history that covered a big part of the western edge of Texas's panhandle.

Texas Jack sez it dates back to when cattle outnumbered people by more than five hundred to one.

 **Y** is for Gil Ybardo, who established Nacogdoches, where most American colonists saw their first Texas settlement.

Z is for Lorenzo De Zavala, Santa Anna's aide who left to join the Texans because he didn't like Santa Anna's methods. He became the first vice president of the Republic of Texas.

Texas Jack sez zatzall.